CLOSER

Letters From A Loving Father
Unwavering, Unmatched, and
Unconditional Love

Devotional and Prayer Journal

CLOSER

"The more I know of Him, the more I know of myself"

~Michelle K. Patterson

CLOSER

Letters From A Loving Father

Devotional and Prayer Journal

Vol.1

MICHELLE K. PATTERSON

Foreword by Jamila Pleas

Closer
by Michelle Patterson

Published by Michelle K. Patterson

Copyright 2019 by Michelle K. Patterson

ISBN: 978-0-578-49489-0

Cover design by Kentyla Art Designs
Page layout design by Ty Young – Young Dreams Publications
Edited by Karen Ratliff, 365Consultinggroup.com

Printed in the United States of America

DEDICATION

To anyone who doubts that God really exists, I've doubted too. To anyone who is seeking to know why they exist on earth and their purpose for being alive, I've sought to know why I exist as well. To anyone who has said, "I know that there has to be more to life than this?" I've said the same thing. Lastly, if there is someone who may be longing for a deeper connection with God - I yearn for God as well. If any of these areas describe you, I've got great news! He wants to have a more intimate relationship with you. In fact, this journal is written especially for you.

The purpose of this journal is to lead you into a closer, more intimate relationship with God, and to reveal the Father's love in a greater magnitude. The more you know of Him, the more you will know of yourself. Only then can your true destiny be revealed and fulfilled.

"The kingdom of heaven is like treasure hidden in a field, which a man found and covered up. Then in His joy he goes and sells all that he has and buys that field" (Matthew 13:44).

ACKNOWLEDGMENTS

Thank you to my Lord and Savior Jesus Christ, without Your guidance, none of this would be possible. The joy of the Lord has been my strength. To my remarkable and supportive husband, Ojo Patterson - who gives me so much love and support. Actually, you "OJO" are my biggest hero! Your Godly wisdom and determination is what helps me to keep moving forward. I'm thankful for our children Pra'Vione, A'Maginese, and Malik for always believing in me, and rooting for me to succeed. You all are my gift from God and my greatest inheritance.

To my mom and dad, Margo and Harold Clay- your prayers and guidance kept me safe and secure as a child. Your tough love is just what I needed at times to cause me to rise to a higher standard.To my dearest sister, Myra Winding-Hermann, thank you for giving me encouraging words and reminding me of what you've always seen in me. You admonished me to just "step out on faith."

To my other mom In-Love, Kenisha Patterson, Momma Marie, and my extended family, thank you for embracing me as your very own and loving me.

To my closest and dearest friends, Faith, Annaliza, Jamila, Monica, and LaDonna, who have stood alongside me, nudging me to keep writing, to keep fighting, and to keep focus - your friendship helped me to get through my toughest seasons.

In closing, I'm grateful for everyone who has sown seeds into my life along life's journey to help bring forth this harvest.

FOREWORD
by Jamila Pleas

Psalms 3:5 *"I lie down and sleep, I wake again,
because the Lord sustains me."*

In this scripture, David's faith was his anchor in a time of uncertainty and attack. Instead of wrestling with anxiety, he was able to sleep in the midst of trouble because of his confidence in God to deliver him. As we draw closer to God, He gives us a rest that is undisturbed by our wavering emotions, life circumstances, prior mistakes, or experiences. The Lord will quiet the still waters. Like the ocean, the surface is quiet and still, but underneath this stillness is a force of waves and currents. In my own ocean of tears shed while overcoming depression and the pressures of being a single mom, I was able to find comfort by beginning to know God as a loving Father. I am always grateful that during this time of building my faith, the Lord brought Michelle Patterson into my life.

Michelle provided a sense of community, encouragement, and a voice that reminded me of God's promises. In this volume, you now have a sampling of what I have gained from Michelle. You will gain a knowledge of God's word and promises that will allow His grace to empower you to draw closer to the well that never runs dry. Over the next 14 days, you will experience the love of the Father and begin to be free to move into purpose. It is my prayer that the words will come alive, you will draw closer in relationship with the Father and find a rest that allows you to cease from trying to make things happen in your own strength, learning once and for all how sweet it is to wholly lean on God.

There is safety in His presence. Let your journey to becoming CLOSER begin.

INTRODUCTION

You didn't ask to come into this world, right? However, we were all developed in our mother's womb. Did we have a say in the matter, no? It is just what it is. We can settle for that notion, or we can choose to believe that we were all destined to be here. I don't believe any inventor creates anything without a purpose in mind. So, before we were ever created in our mother's womb, God had a plan for you and me.

Somewhere, after conception and entering into the world, we were shaped by our environment and experiences. Most people have come face to face with pain, disappointment, rejection, fear, neglect, and even trauma. Our human instincts cause us to do whatever is necessary to protect ourselves, usually mistrust is one of the first responders. Then, without even realizing it, we build walls around us. These walls don't allow anything to get in, not even the things that are beneficial for us. For instance, we reject love. However, the good news is that we have a loving Father who is longing for us to know how much He loves us.

CLOSER

DAY 1

My Child,

Take a moment to reflect on how far you've come. You will always be loved by Me. No matter what you've been told by others, or how you may think of yourself, I love you and I will be with you wherever you go. There is so much liberation in knowing how much you are loved. The enemy has been fighting you your whole life to prevent you from ever knowing the truth about Me. He wanted to distract you from ever realizing your true identity in Me, Jesus Christ. Today, I want you to know that you've never been alone, I've been pursuing you your whole life. I'm extending my hand, beckoning you to come closer.

"For God so loved the world, that He gave his only begotten Son, that whoever believes in Him should not perish but have eternal life." John 3:16 ESV.

PRAYER

Father, I want to experience your love. I haven't always felt Your presence, but I've seen evidence of Your presence in my life. Father, forgive me for shutting You out. I willingly surrender my heart to receive Your love. I accept Your invitation to enter into a closer relationship with You, which will lead me into eternal life. Amen.

DAY 2

I'm attracted to your weaknesses. When you are weak, I'm made strong in you. You have no reason to be ashamed. You were created in My image; by Me, and for Me. I have set you apart for My purpose to bring glory to My name. The more you learn of Me, the more you will know of yourself. I send you My Helper, the Holy Spirit (also known as "the Comforter") in My name, to lead you, teach you, and to remind you of everything I have spoken.

"But He said unto me, My grace is sufficient for you, for my power is made perfect in weakness. Therefore I will boast all the more gladly in my weaknesses, so that the power of Christ may rest upon me" (2 Corinthians 12: 9) ESV.

PRAYER

Father, I'm no longer ashamed because You are gracious forgive me. I confess my sins and turn from them. I've distanced myself from You at times because I felt so unworthy of Your love. Today, I accept Your forgiveness, and by faith, I receive Your power to be healed. Amen.

CLOSER

DAY 3

Come closer and learn of Me. For I know the plans I have for you, to prosper you, not to harm you, but to bring you to an expected end. In Me, you will find rest, believe in Me and you will be blessed. For one path leads to life, while the other leads to death and destruction. Choose life. I am near, draw nearer to Me. Take My hand and I will lead you into green pastures, beside still waters, and restore your soul.

"And if you faithfully obey the voice of the Lord your God, being careful to do all His commandments that I command you today, the Lord God will set you high above all the nations of the earth" (Deuteronomy 28:1).

PRAYER

Dear Lord, In You is where I find peace. I want to draw nearer, but I allow the demands of life to distract me from spending time with You. Please forgive me. Today, I will make haste to find a space, wait patiently, and listen to Your voice. I am yours. Amen.

CLOSER

DAY 4

If I call you, will you come? When you cry out to Me, I answer you expediently. Why do you delay, and do not obey My instructions? Cease from your own works and follow Me. Many are the plans in a person's heart, but it is My purpose that will stand. Turn back to your first love - My arms are outstretched. I'm here to receive you, and I will remain with you. I am yours forever. I invite you to come away with Me, your bride-groom awaits. Come closer.

"And I am sure of this, that He who began a good work in you will bring it to completion at the day of Jesus Christ" (Philippians 1:6).

PRAYER

My Protector, I've put my trust in things that are temporary, instead of putting my trust in You, the One who created me and gave Himself for me. The pleasures of this life have consumed me. I didn't realize that I've strayed far away from You. Today, I turn back to my First- Love. I commit my work to you, Lord, so that my plans will be established. Amen

DAY 5

You will face many challenges in this world that will make you question My existence and your purpose for being born. You were no mistake. I knew you before you were formed in your mother's womb. The world has many counterfeit, but the truth is I am the One and Only true and living God. You were born to manifest my glory on the earth. Your true purpose is found in Me, the more you learn of Me, the more you will know of yourself.

"I am the vine; you are the branches. Whoever abides in Me and I in him, he will bear much fruit, for apart from Me you can do nothing" (John 15:5).

PRAYER

Father, there are times when I feel so far from You and overwhelmed with life's demands. Help me to remember; "not by might, neither by power, but by Your Spirit." Your grace is sufficient for me, and Your Word will guide me into all truth. On days that I feel disconnected, help me to remember that if I stay connected to You, my joy will remain. Amen

DAY 6

Are you living? Life isn't just merely existing, but it embodies the fullness of who I am. You cannot comprehend or grasp the vastness of that fullness. However, it is your inheritance. You can't continue to dwell on your past faults or mistakes. New life awaits you. Take up your wings and fly like an eagle. You will reach greater heights once you have removed the limitations that you have placed on yourself and me. I am giving you clear lenses so that you will see yourself as I see you. You are made in my image, and your beauty exceeds any superficial beliefs that you have of yourself. It is time to arise. Arise and allow your light to shine.

"You make known to me the path of life; in your presence there is fullness of joy; at your right hand are pleasures forever more" (Psalms 16:11)

PRAYER

My Lord, I long to be in Your presence. When I seek You with a whole heart, I will never be disappointed, for You will show me your hidden treasures. I will abide in You so that You may abide in me and lead me on the path that is sure. I want to dwell with You forevermore. Your presence is where I find peace and rest. Amen.

CLOSER

DAY 7

Arise! Your light has come. I came to remind you of the light which dwells within you. Why have you hidden in the shadows? Whenever you are present, darkness cannot remain because of how beautiful you are! How long will you refrain from embracing the truth? Have you forgotten that you are made in My image? You are an heir of God and whatever belongs to Me now belongs to you. It's time that you walk in your true identity. Arise!

"For Zion's sake, I will not keep silent, and for Jerusalem's sake I will not be quiet, until her righteousness goes forth as brightness, and her salvation as a burning torch. The nations shall see your righteousness, and all the kings your glory, and you shall be called by a new name that the mouth of the Lord will give" (Isaiah 62:1-2).

PRAYER

Father, when darkness is all around me, help me to remember that You dwell within me. Your Light shines through me, and I am called to be light in dark places. Amen.

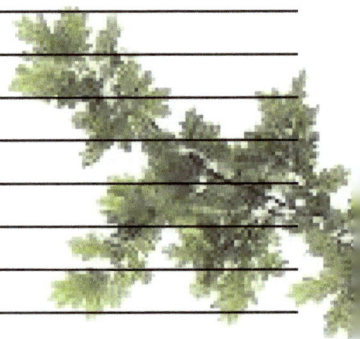

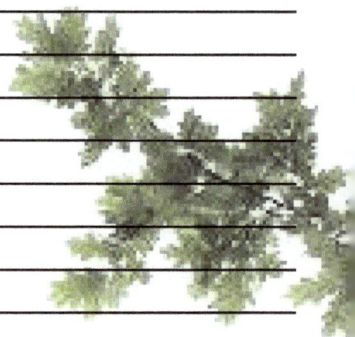

CLOSER

DAY 8

I know every part of you. I am with you always. Though you may face many trials and be persecuted for my namesake, I am here in your suffering. The world does not know Me, but you know Me. Don't allow the troubles and cares of this world to lead you far from Me, instead draw nearer than you have before. You will need My strength to carry you and my guidance to keep your feet from stumbling. When you call upon Me, I will answer, and the whole world will know that you belong to Me. Put your trust in Me, and you will never be put to shame.

"Truly, I say to you, whoever says to this mountain; be taken up and thrown into the sea, and does not doubt in his heart, but believes that what he says will come to pass, it will be done for him. Therefore, I tell you, whatever you ask in prayer, believe that you have received it, and it will be yours" (Mark 11:23-24).

PRAYER

Dear Lord, the truth is, I can't always see Your hand upon my life. I want to believe Your Word, but sometimes I doubt it. Please help me Lord with my unbelief. I want to learn to trust You with my whole heart. Amen.

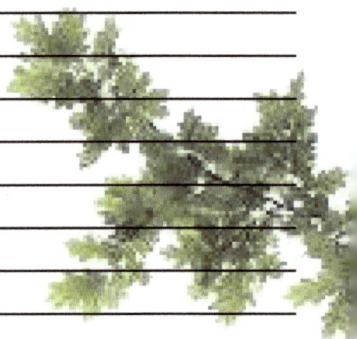

CLOSER

DAY 9

Patiently wait for Me. I'm calling you to come and sit at My feet, to learn of Me, and adapt My ways. You can't attempt to do anything in My name without being sent. I love you My child. The closer you come, the more peace you will find. I have hidden treasures that you know not of, neither does the world know. I have hidden them before the foundation of the world. I have beckoned many to come and sit at my table. However, many refuse to come. I will allow you to partake in the wedding ceremony. You are my bride.

"For God has not given us a Spirit of fear; but of power, and of love, and of a sound mind" (2 Timothy 1:7).

PRAYER

Father, grant me patience, while I wait. Give me the understanding and knowledge of Your ways. I will sit at Your feet, and cast all of my cares there. When I arise, I will have strength, and when I lay down to sleep I will have peace. Lord, I am grateful for Your grace that is sufficient in my time of need. I hasten to sit at your table, Father, and partake in the wedding feast. Amen.

CLOSER

DAY 10

Oh, how I am mindful of you. I can number the hair strands on your head. you are unique, and there will never be another you. Beautiful is your name, despite your flaws, you are perfectly made! Laugh at calamity and lift up your voice like a trumpet. Sound the alarm and warn my people that I am alive and I'm not dead. Look around you at the evidence of my glory, my majesty, and my power. Fear not, I have preserved you, you are my handy work, and all will marvel at your sight. Selah

"Great are the works of the Lord, studied by all who delight in them. Full of splendor and majesty is His work and His righteousness endures forever" (Psalms 111: 2-3).

PRAYER

Oh Lord, My heart longs for You and no one can mend it, but you. I am broken and shattered, but I was told that You can create masterpieces. You are the potter; I am the clay, mold me as You please. Here I am Lord, create in me a clean heart and renew the right Spirit in me. Amen.

CLOSER

DAY 11

At the dawn of each day, I stand and watch as your eyes open wide, wondering if you will even notice that I am present. I anticipate hearing you call my name. I wait patiently while you struggle to break free from the business of your day, to come away with Me. Incline your ear to Me, discover new possibilities and learn of the plans that I have for your future. Take my hand and follow Me.

"On the glorious splendor of Your majesty and on Your wondrous works, I will meditate" (Psalms 145:5).

PRAYER

Lord, You are here with me from the time that I wake up until the going down of the sun. I long to be in Your presence because in Your presence I find rest. I will answer when You call me to come away with You because you know what I have need of. Thank you for Your mercies each day. Forgive me for putting You last. I honor You and put You first, above anything else from this day forward. Amen

DAY 12

Keep My promises in your heart. Surely, if I say, "I will never leave you," I never will. When you go about your day and you are faced with decisions, know that I am here. Ask of Me anything and I will answer you. You won't always agree, but you must obey. My ways are not your ways, and My thoughts are higher than your thoughts. Put your trust in me, knowing that My way will preserve you. I'm your Father and I know what's best for you. Then, you will see My majesty and the wonderful display of My power working in your life. Many will be in awe and glorify Me. My child, I will never withhold any good thing from you. I am working in your patience and creating in you a clean heart so that you will steward well, whatever I give you.

"Can a woman forget her nursing child that she should have no compassion on the son of her womb?" Even these may forget, yet I will not forget you" (Isaiah 49:15).

PRAYER

Oftentimes, I forget to ask You for directions. In fact, I deliberately keep some things far from You (at least I imagine I do), but You are all knowing. Father, I realize that I've placed myself in great danger because I refused to listen. Sometimes it's hurtful when I'm chastised by You, but I know that's what a loving Father does. Father, forgive me for doubting You and resisting Your hand. Please guide me and teach me Your ways because without Your guidance and wisdom, I would face utter destruction. If I remain under your covering, there is safety in You.

DAY 13

You can live an abundant life because all of your sins are forgiven. In fact, I remember them no more. Don't dwell on your past of what "so -and so" has done to you, or how you've fallen short of my instructions. Everyone has fallen short of my glory, and all have sinned. The good news is that you are no longer a slave to sin or your past life.

If you confess with your mouth that Jesus is Lord and believe in your heart that God has raised Him from the dead, you will be saved (Romans 10:9). For everyone who calls on the name of the Lord will be saved (Romans 10:13). You must not live your life with regret. I've taken every mistake and circumstance you've experienced, and I'm using them to tell "your story." You will testify to the world about My love and how I made you free.

So, My child, it is time for you to start "living!" I've delivered you out of the darkness and brought you into My marvelous light. Today, just as I live, you live!

"And he said to her, "your sins are forgiven" (Luke 7: 48).

PRAYER

Now, that I know You have been with me my whole life and You were carrying me every step of the way, I have the strength to keep going. I had no hope and no desire to live, but You thought enough of me to come after me. Even if my earthly father falls short of loving me, You pick up the pieces and give me beauty for shes. I no longer want to resist Your love. Give me a new heart, and come and dwell here forever. Amen.

CLOSER

DAY 14

My Beloved,

When you enter into the land that I promised you, remember Me. Hide My words in your heart and never forget them. You will be tempted to leave Me, or distance yourself from Me. I admonish you to commune with Me daily. Seek Me with your whole heart because I won't always strive with you.

Extend love to your brothers and sisters, just as I have extended my grace and love to you. Forgive quickly, just as I have forgiven you. You will always be the apple of My eye, and there is nothing that you can ever do to separate you from my love. I chose you, you didn't choose Me. You are My most treasured gift and I long to abide in you, and you in Me. I am your first love, and I will always be.

"Delight yourself in the Lord, and He will give you the desires of your heart. Commit your way to the Lord; trust him, and he will act. He will bring forth your righteousness as the light" (Proverbs 37:4-6)

PRAYER

Father, I can't imagine walking this journey alone. Now, I'm confident that with the strength of God, I can do anything. If I become weary, I will call upon Your name. Your love is an anchor for me. In fact, I was merely existing, and I wasn't living at all. Your words lift me up and give me hope and purpose for living. Lord when you reach for me or call upon my name, I will come closer. Today, I surrender my life completely.

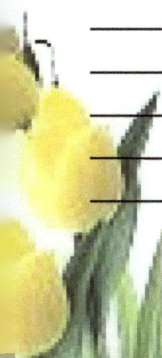

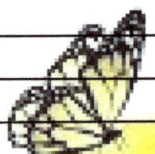

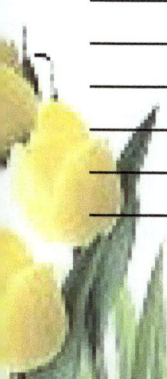

A Letter From The Author

Dear Reader,

I want you to know that you did not receive this book, by chance. I've been praying for you. You are embarking upon the greatest journey of your life. The pursuit of happiness begins with contentment in God. Your love story is being reborn. Keep drawing CLOSER to Him, and he will draw CLOSER to you. Pray and meditate on the word of God each day, which is the Holy Bible. Talk to him each day, just like you have through this journal. Your heavenly Father is listening.

My Child…

I am the way, the truth, and the life. No one comes to the father, except by me (Jesus Christ). Come… (John 14:6)

With Love,

Michelle K. Patterson

ABOUT THE AUTHOR

Over 18 years ago, Michelle K. Patterson encountered God in a way that changed her life forever. She vowed to share her experience with whomever she could. Her story has been shared with thousands, mostly through outreach efforts. Her life is a demonstration of God's redemptive love, power, and resurrection.

Michelle's mission is to reach the nations by sharing the Gospel of Jesus Christ through her writing, music, teaching, and preaching. She has seen, first-hand, how lives and communities are being transformed by way of the Holy Spirit and the Word of God.

In addition, there are two important keys that she lives by: "Building Relationships" and "Getting Involved." She believes faith must be put into action and we must be the change we want to see.

Michelle Patterson lives with her husband Ojo Patterson and their three amazing children; Pra'Vione, A'Maginese, and Malik.

Write the Author
Email: Michelle@beautywithintranscends.com

www.ingramcontent.com/pod-product-compliance
Lightning Source LLC
Chambersburg PA
CBHW051234090426
42740CB00001B/16